The Way of the Cross

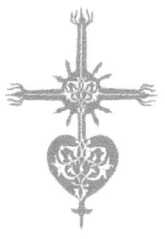

Mary Jane Miller

STATIONS OF THE CROSS: Paintings and Meditations
by Mary Jane Miller
www.millericons.com

All paintings by Mary Jane Miller.
EDITOR: Rev Canon George F. Woodward III.
ASSISTANT EDITOR: Laila Bárcenas Meade
BOOK & COVER DESIGN: Mary Meade

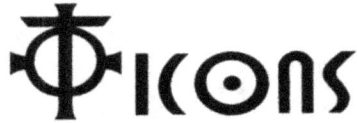

© 2019 Mary Jane Miller. All rights reserved.
ISBN 979839911852

All rights reserved. No part of this publication may be reproduced Stored in a retrieval system or transmitted, in any from or by any means electronic mechanical, recording or otherwise without prior permission from copyright holder.

Introduction

THE WAY OF THE CROSS evotional practice was establishedin the thirteenth century. They use the ritual metaphorically to journey with him from his trial to his entombment. The participants stand before snap shot images to immerse themselves in the story of Jesus Christ's final sufferings as he walked to Mount Calvary. The road between his condemnation at court and final crucifixion is known as the Via Dolorosa ("Way of Sorrows") or Via Crucis ("Way of the Cross"). In Jerusalem it is still walked by many pilgrims today.

Via Crucis is exemplary not of one man's walk on one historic day, but the walk for all humanity. The idea is not to become Christ but to gain the awareness of the human condition and come to the conclusion, " If Christ has done it so can I."

For two millenniums the human circumstance has changed little, we all still suffer, we all still feel abandoned and we all still get betrayed. Migrant workers, soldiers, prisoners, racial discrimination and violence, the poor and the homeless, the grieving, and the mentally ill are among the many people we will meet along the path. When we focus our mind and heart on the "way" we realize there is strength in His example whatever the circumstances.

Lent is comprised of the 40 days before Easter, a season devoted to deep examination and reflection on self. From the earliest of days of Christianity, followers of Jesus told the story of his passion, death and resurrection. Pilgrims arriving in Jerusalem were anxious to see the sites where Jesus walked. As Christianity took root around the globe, these holy sites were too distant for many to travel to. By the 1500's, communities all over the world started creating "replicas" of the places along the route to Calvary in Jerusalem. Eventually, these shrines became the 14 stations celebrate.

Why they are named The Way of the Cross'

You may be wondering why the sites are called Stations of the Cross. The word station comes from the Latin word meaning to stand. We are walking from Christ's trial to His crucifixion at Calvary and we stop and stand to commemorate various moments illustrating what took place along the way. As you come to each station, you stand with those who originally stood and watched as Christ passed by on route to His death. At each station you stop, read the scriptures, pray the prayers, and contemplate the situation before moving on. As you walk from one station to the next, your walking becomes a devotional act, because you are walking with Jesus as He walks to Calvary. Our book illustrates the series of 14 images, with the15th added as the culmination of the tradition and final fruition of all the suffering.

Why did you forsake me?... To what purpose?... The stations speak of injustice with no mercy, they speak of Jesus's journey to his death with no complaint. But along the way there is not one death but many, each station revealing a kind of death of self and surrender to the horrors life has given us. We are supported by a few on lookers but ultimately we like Christ have to endure seemingly alone what is happening in our life. This is not just the historical reenactment, but the pilgrimage for all humanity until we learn to not do harm to one another.

Sacred Art is more than Biblical Story Telling

Sacred Art is more than biblical story telling. Rituals like the Stations of the cross were designed as a visual tool for the community. They help us navigate through a prescribed set of messages and motif and are no longer limited to only church. While the traditional form retains the rich connotations of the underlying message, there is room for reinterpretations that traverse boundaries and expand the possibility of transforming our normal life. The Stations of the Cross allow the inquiry for why do we have to suffer including the social, political, and metaphysical ways as well.

My small collection strips the elements in the story to faces, hands and the cross to underscore our human commonality. The Stations exalt the unjust suffering, particularly those individuals struggling against authority. Parts of each one of us are seen, touched and crucified everyday.

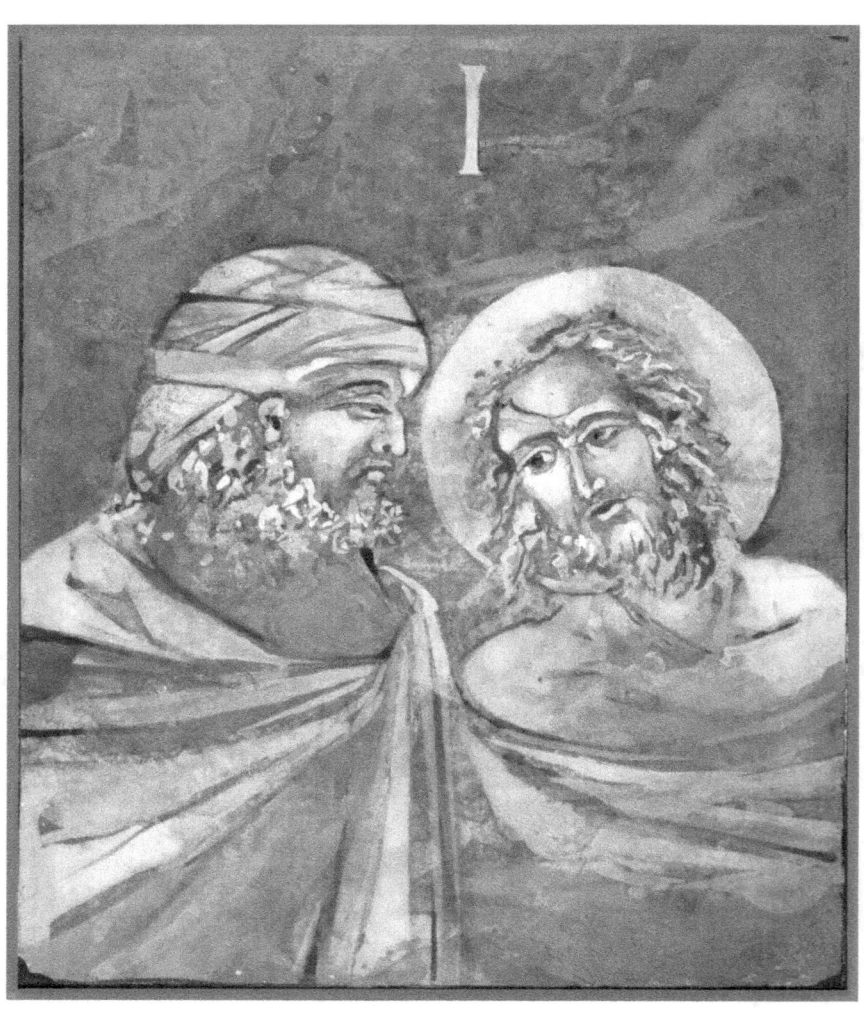

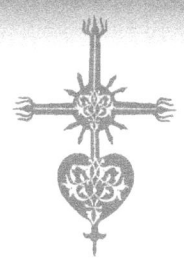

STATION 1:
Jesus is Condemned to Death

WE ADORE YOU, O Christ, and we bless you.
BECAUSE BY YOUR HOLY cross you have redeemed the world.

Jesus is betrayed by the people in authority. He stands before Pilate as a spiritual warrior, vulnerable in the face of evil force, dominance and power. Haven't we all known betrayal? We want a certain outcome and end up with another. The intellectual stamina needed to not resist at times like this is enormous, to allow the injustice, accept condemnation without opposition and without want. He has said, "Yes," to God and placed his life in God's hands, reminding Pilate, "You have nothing in your hands."

We follow Jesus with reverence, praying for our willingness to surrender and trust that there is a plan unfolding and to submit willingly without fear. We cannot resist because it is out of our control, beyond the reach of our ignorance and fear. We walk with Jesus in the direction someone else has chosen. We cannot argue nor resist.

> *Almighty God, whose most dear Son went not up to joy, but first suffered pain, and entered into glory before he was crucified, mercifully grant that we, walking in the way of the cross, may find it none other than the way of life and peace, through Jesus Christ your Son, our Lord. Amen.*

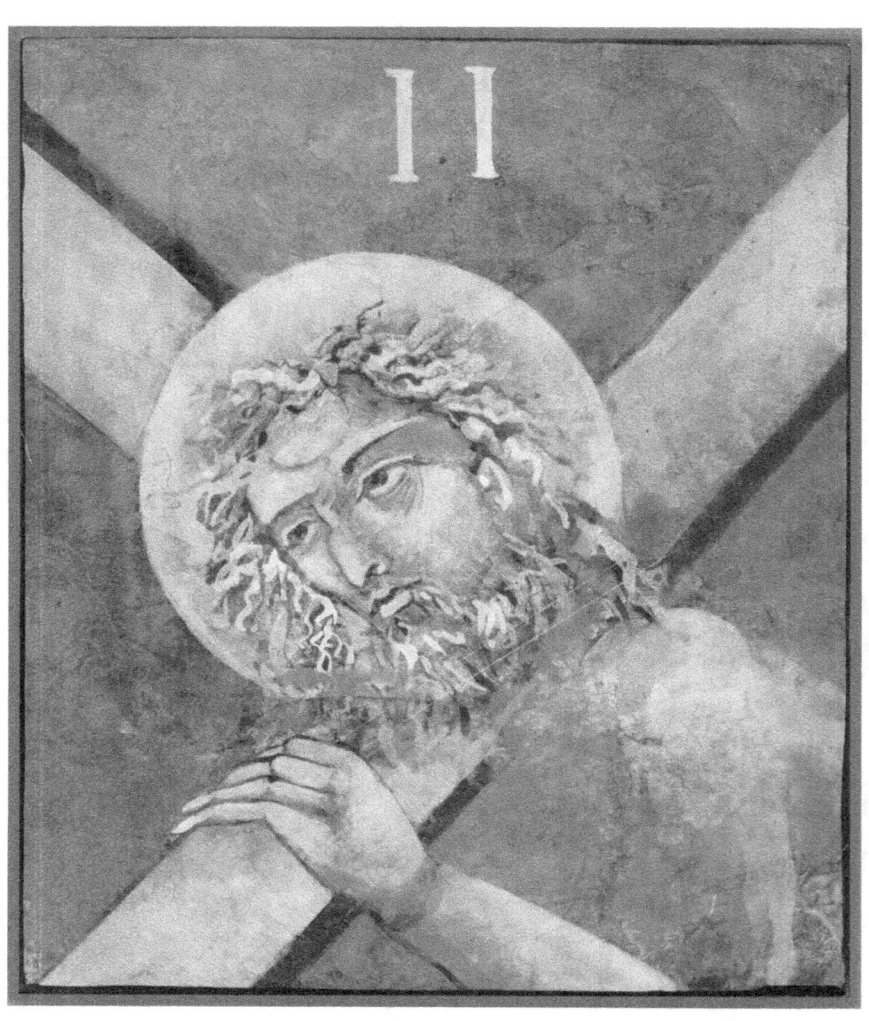

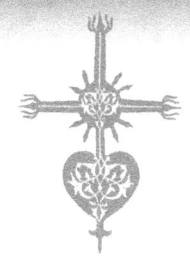

STATION 2

Jesus Takes Up the Cross

WE ADORE YOU, O Christ, and we bless you.
BECAUSE BY YOUR HOLY cross you have redeemed the world.

Jesus receives the heavy rough wooden cross that he will be crucified on. He took the weight of injustice upon his shoulders! The wood symbolizes his connection to earth and to humanity. With each step, he unites himself to our human experience and teaches us to not turn away from injustice, but instead, to stare at it without flinching. He accepts the path of human misery and suffering that is part of our human life and shows us how to say "yes".

Each and every one of us has a cross to carry. Whether beset by illness, emotional turmoil, physical deformity or other burdens, each of us must carry on with what we have been given. No one can walk for us. There will be no short cuts, or payback. John 21:18: "...but when you are old, you will stretch out your hands, and another will dress you and carry you where you do not want to go."

> *Almighty God, whose beloved Son willingly endured the agony and shame of the cross for our redemption: give us courage to take up our cross and follow him, who lives and reigns for ever and ever. Amen.*

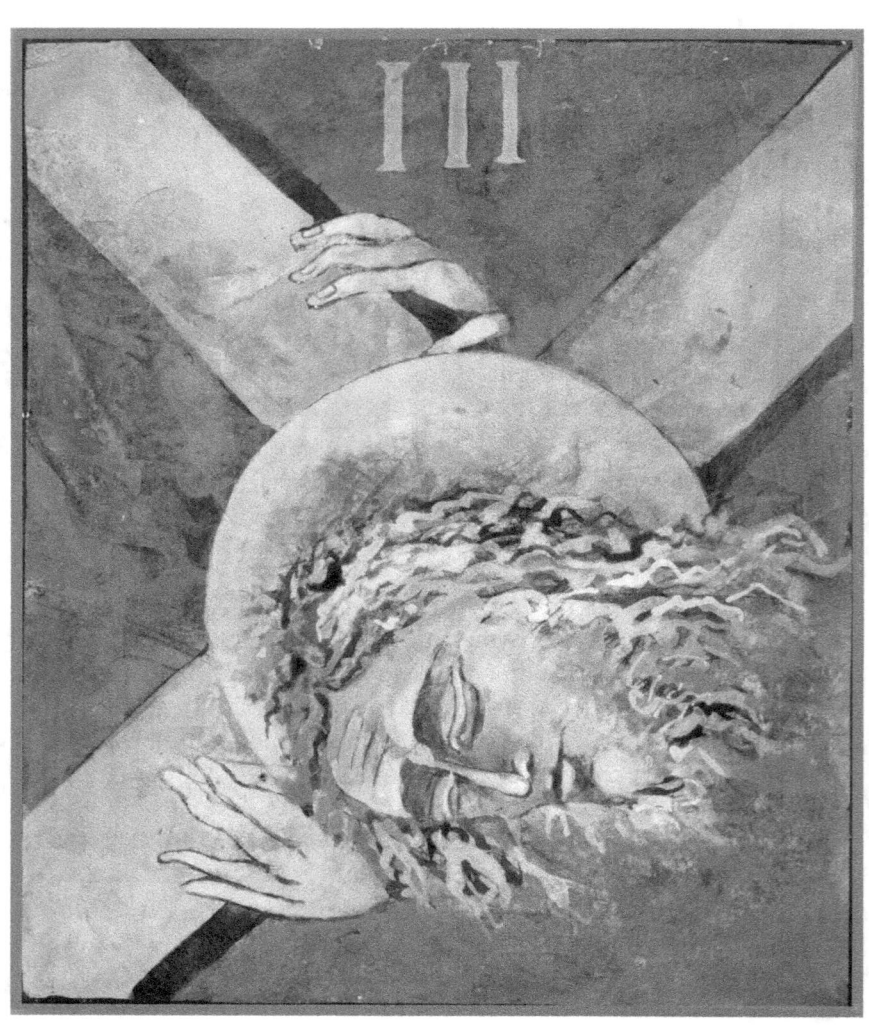

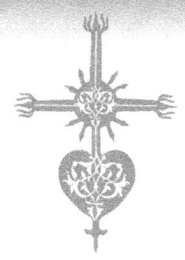

STATION 3

Jesus Falls for the First Time

WE ADORE YOU, O Christ, and we bless you.
BECAUSE BY YOUR HOLY cross you have redeemed the world.

Christ lies on the ground in weakness, beneath unfair burdens. He knows this should not be happening. His resignation is shown in quiet dignity. He feels powerless, wondering if he will be able to continue. He is pulled up and forced to continue. We watch him stand again and gain inner strength in spite of the clash he must feel between tolerance and frustration. Christ is suffering for a cause not fully understood by any of those around him. He hears the expressions of hatred in the crowd. He does not shield himself, rather, endures the pain without expression. He falls down out of sheer exhaustion and fear.

We all face times of grief. We want to give up and surrender, but we know no one can walk for us or carry the choices we have made. We rest with Christ in succumbing to the burden of life.

Surely he has borne our griefs, And carried our sorrows

> O you know us to be set in the midst of so many and great dangers that by reason of the frailty of our nature we cannot always stand upright: grant us such strength and protection as may support us in all dangers and carry us through all temptations, through Christ our Lord. Amen.

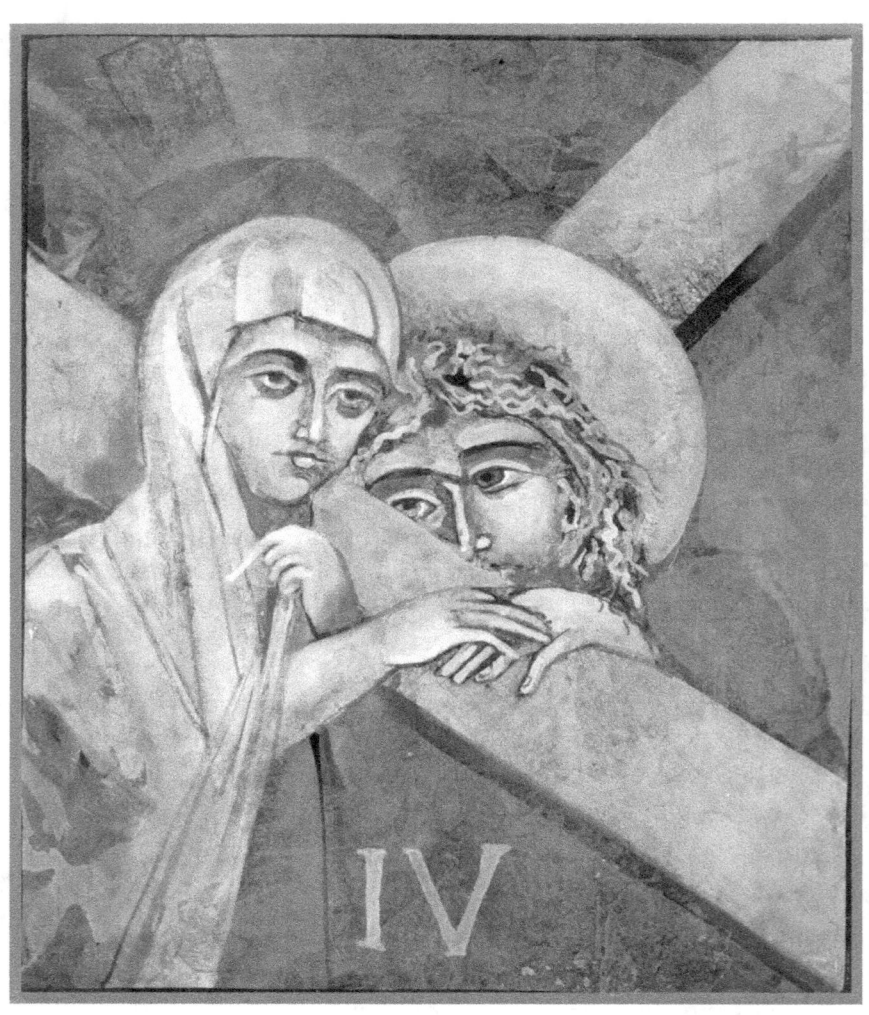

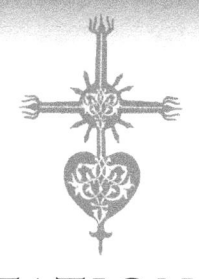

STATION 4

Jesus Encounters His Afflicted Mother

WE ADORE YOU, O Christ, and we bless you.
BECAUSE BY YOUR HOLY cross you have redeemed the world.

Every mother has memories of her early relationship with her newborn. Christ is being seen by his mother up close for the last time. Their loving glance is captured in one moment. Christ is facing death through the inescapable, unjust torture that is unfolding. Jesus path allows him one last encounter with his mother, the powerful source of strength throughout his life. She taught him the meaning of the words, "Be it done unto me." Now they look into each other's eyes. He is pained to see his mother's tears of sorrow and helplessness at the sight of him. She almost smiles, blessing his mission through her love and trust of God's love which will eternally bind them together.

Our betrayals are intense and softened only when we realize we are loved. At this moment along the journey, we remember the times we have been seen up close and intimate, even if briefly.

A sword will pierce your own soul also. And fill your heart with bitter pain.

> O God, who willed that in the passion of your Son a sword of grief should pierce the soul of the Blessed Mary, his mother: mercifully grant that your Church, having shared with her in his passion, may be made worthy to share in the joys of his resurrection, who lives and reigns for ever and ever. Amen.

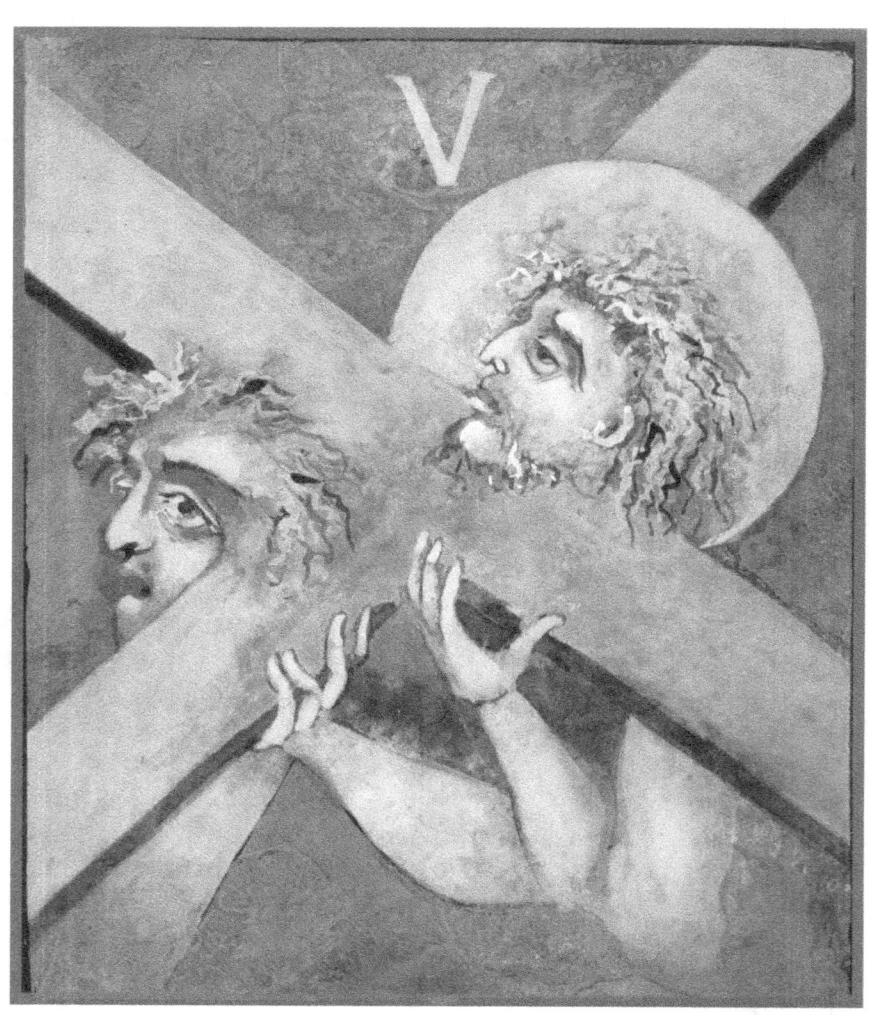

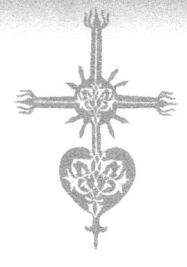

STATION 5

Simon of Cyrene Takes Up the Cross

WE ADORE YOU, O Christ, and we bless you.
BECAUSE BY YOUR HOLY cross you have redeemed the world.

Simon was a young African boy from Cyrene, in northern Africa. The Cyreneaic Jews had a synagogue in Jerusalem where many went for the annual feasts. Any Jew might feel the touch of the flat sword or spear from a Roman soldier and know that his service was demanded, that he had no choice but to comply. That is what likely happened to Simon of Cyrene when he was told to bear the cross for Jesus. Scholars believe that it was then when Simon converted to Christianity, following this chance encounter with Jesus.

Jesus is humble and weak, and not able to carry this whole burden alone and humbly accepts the help given.

Simon's service reminds us to do the right thing. It is better to serve than be served. This one man was chosen to come into discipleship and relationship with him, an opportunity to share the journey. In standing here, we choose his journey and commit ourselves to Jesus and "The Way." John 16:32: "A time is coming, and in fact has come, when you will be scattered, each to your own home. You will leave me all alone. Yet I am not alone, for my Father is with me."

"Whoever does not bear his own cross and come after me cannot be my disciple."

> Heavenly Father, whose Son came not to be served but to serve: bless all who, following in his steps, give themselves to the service of others, that with wisdom, patience, and courage they may minister to the suffering, the friendless, and the needy, for the love of him who laid down his life for us. Amen.

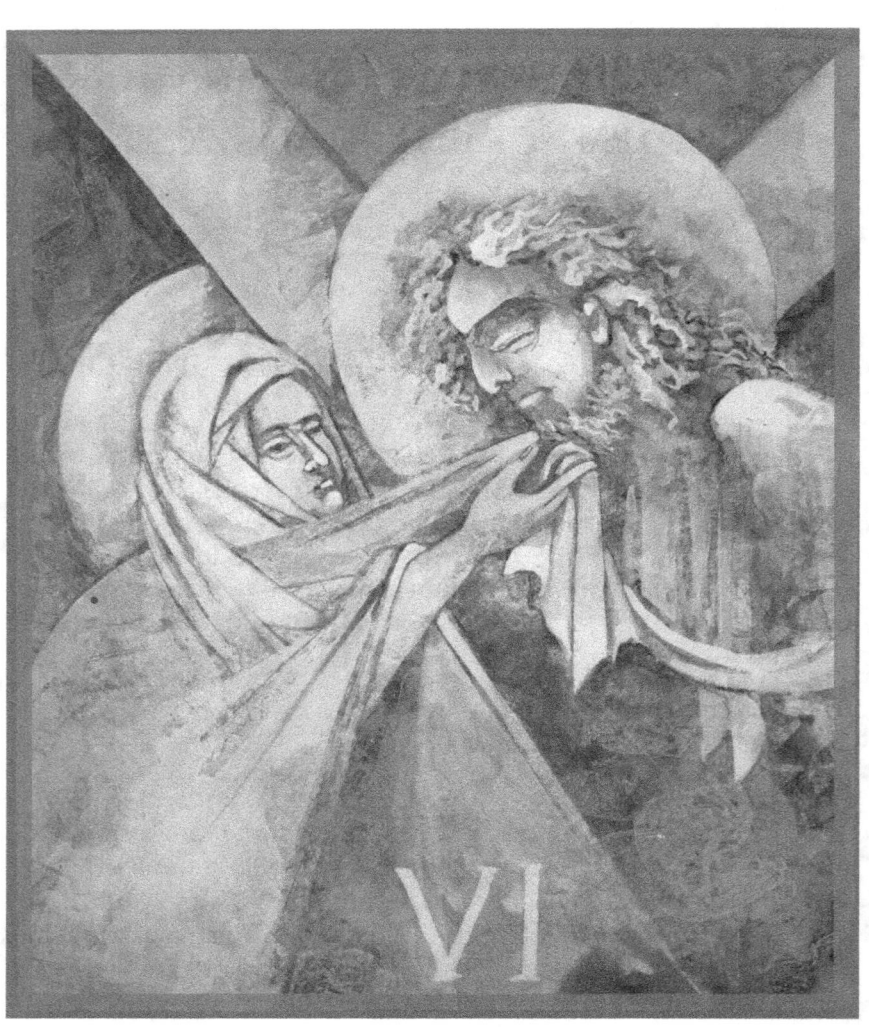

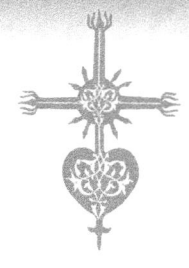

STATION 6

Veronica Wipes Christ's Face

WE ADORE YOU, O Christ, and we bless you.
BECAUSE BY YOUR HOLY cross you have redeemed the world.

Veronica may have been a women of privilege, living out an established place in society. She knows how to serve and does not shrink from the everyday drama unfolding before her. It may be her normal behavior to involve herself in the horrible injustices of the time. She responds to those in need saying,"'Here I am Lord; is it I Lord? I have heard your calling in the night."

Jesus' journey is brutal. He has been whipped and beaten. His face shows the signs of his solidarity with all who have ever suffered injustice through vile, abusive treatment. He cannot escape or avoid the terrible feeling of rejection and injustice. He encounters a compassionate, loving disciple who wipes the vulgar spit and mocking blood from his face. On her veil, she discovers the image of his face, his gift to her, for us to contemplate forever.

His face is the same face of those confronting food scarcity, religious persecution, deportation, gender bias, sexual abuse or any other form of rejection and abandonment. Are we strong enough to see the face of Jesus in those who still suffer unjustly today?

Isaiah 6:8: "Then I heard the voice of the Lord saying, 'Whom shall I send? And who will go for us?' And I said, 'Here am I. Send me!' Restore us, O Lord God of hosts: Show the light of your countenance, and we shall be saved."

> *O God, who before the passion of your only begotten Son revealed his glory upon the holy mountain, grant to us that we, beholding by faith the light of his countenance, may be strengthened to bear our cross, and be changed into his likeness from glory to glory, through Christ our Lord. Amen*

Mary Jane Miller

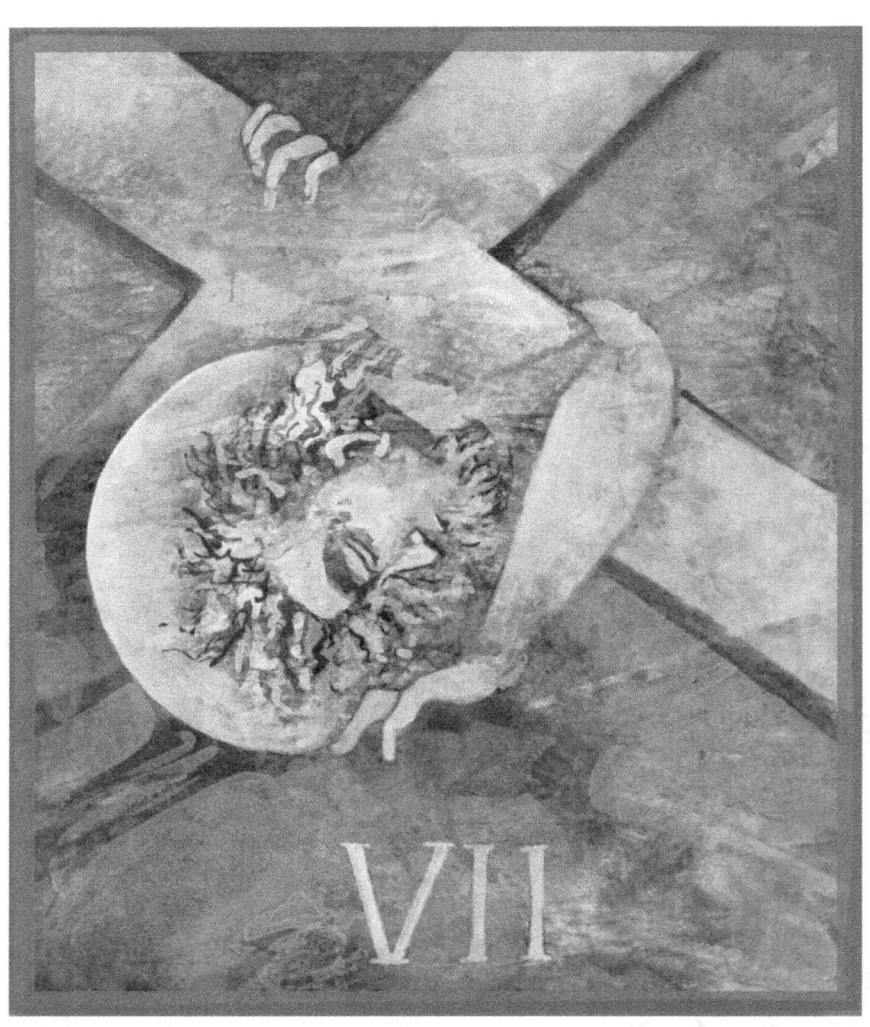

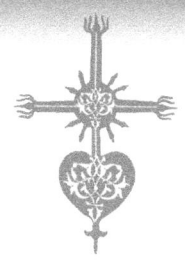

STATION 7

Jesus Falls for the Second Time

WE ADORE YOU, O Christ, and we bless you.
BECAUSE BY YOUR HOLY cross you have redeemed the world.

Jesus has fallen again beneath the weight of unbearable solitude and isolation. He is lost in a nightmare of pain and suffering. His ordeal will not end or be stopped by the crowd who watches on without intervening. The injustice is obvious to the onlookers, who are in a frenzy over having approved something that has gone seriously wrong. It is a growing hysteria of evil that he cannot turn from or change. Even with help, Jesus stumbles and falls to the ground in exhaustion.

He can smell the earth beneath him and feel his own unavoidable death and inevitable separation from earth coming. The moment reminds us that we lead spiritual lives temporarily encapsulated in a human body that roams the earth for a brief time. Genesis 3:19: "...from dust you are and to dust you will return. But as for me, I am a worm and no man, scorned by all and despised by the people."

> *Almighty and ever living God, in your tender love for the human race, you sent your Son our Savior Jesus Christ to take upon him our nature and to suffer death upon the cross, giving us the example of his great humility: mercifully grant that we may walk in the way of his suffering, and also share in his resurrection, he who lives and reigns for ever and ever. Amen.*

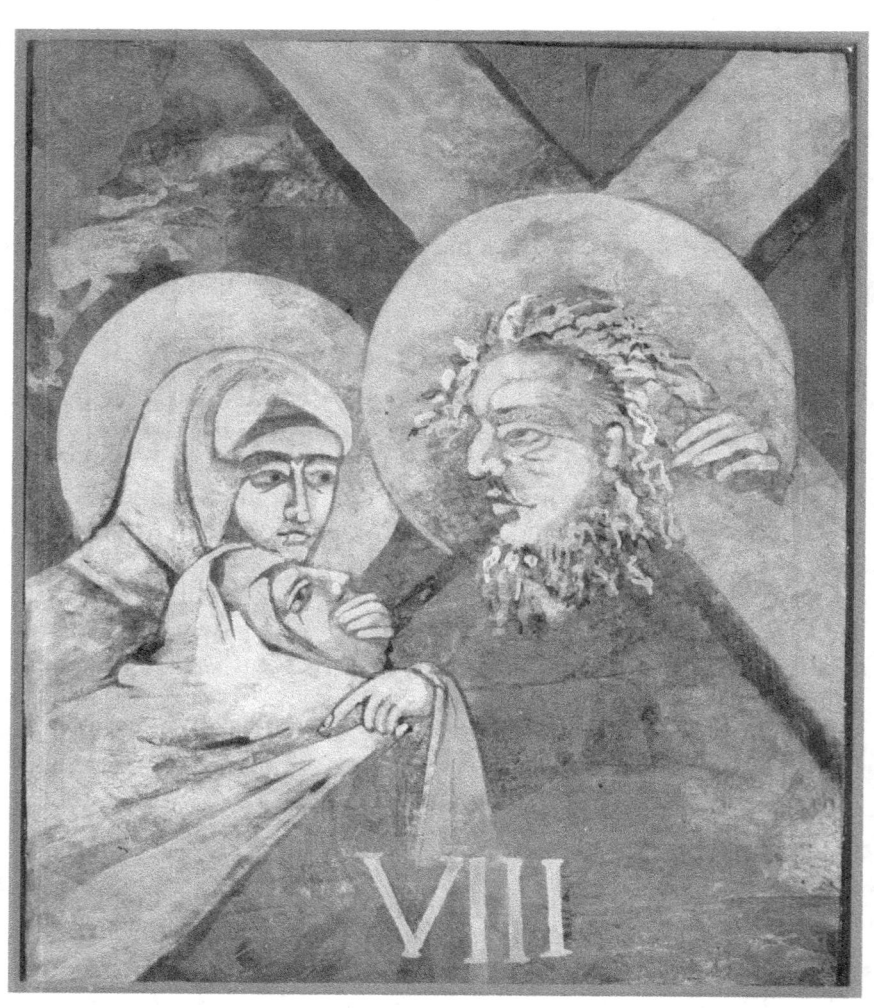

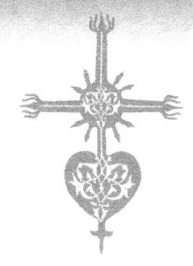

STATION 8

Jesus Meets the Women of Jerusalem

WE ADORE YOU, O Christ, and we bless you.
BECAUSE BY YOUR HOLY cross you have redeemed the world.

Jesus is on his march to death and finds women by his side again for a third time. He has needed and had help along "The Way." He has fallen a few times and now is witness to the anguished faces of the women of Jerusalem. They come out to comfort and thank him. These women have been his friends and witnessed his acts of compassion. He sees them. The decision to stop or walk over to console them is impossible. Their tears are his tears, their heart is his heart.

He has broken all kinds of social and religious conventions to connect with them. Now they are here to support him through this terrible ordeal. He feels their grief, knowing he can't remain with them in this life. He knows they will miss him. Helplessness is something we all feel as we say goodbye or when faced with situations we cannot change. The heart breaks with a yearning for things to be different.

Philippians 4:3: "Yes, and I ask you, my true companion, help these women since they have contended at my side in the cause of the gospel. Those who sowed with tears, will reap with songs of joy."

> Teach your Church, to mourn the sins for which it is guilty, and to repent and forsake them; that by your pardoning grace, the results of our iniquities may not be visited upon our children and our children's children, through Jesus Christ our Lord. Amen.

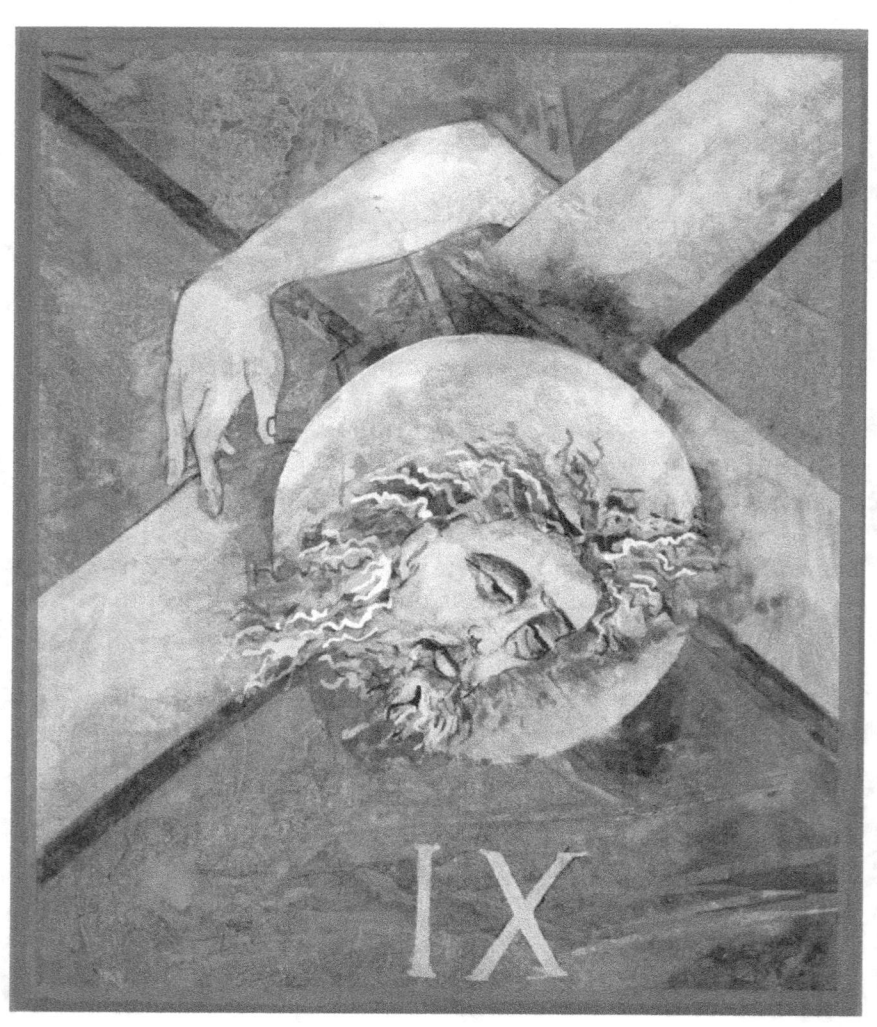

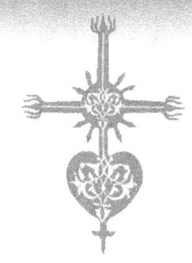

STATION 9

Jesus Falls for the Third Time

WE ADORE YOU, O Christ, and we bless you.
BECAUSE BY YOUR HOLY cross you have redeemed the world.

As you prepare for station 9, let yourself wonder what it must have been like for Jesus walking to his death, a death unimaginable in this day and age. Refugees, prisoners, victims of rape, addiction, child molestation and murder are all intermingled here in the third fall. This last fall is devastating. Jesus can barely proceed to the end. Summoning all his remaining strength he is barely supported by his inner trust in God. Jesus collapses under the weight of the cross. His executioners look at him as a broken man, pathetic, believing he is paying the price he deserves. They pity him and perhaps reluctantly help him up so he can make it up the hill to his own crucifixion.

We cannot change our history. We are trapped by what is happening to us. We know the exhaustion caused by the continual injustice around us. We are weak in our effort to change our directions and attitudes. The law has failed to help us learn to be civilized with one another. Yet as we lay there in exhaustion, we recognize there is a spark of God still breathing and beating within us.

John 16:32: "A time is coming and in fact has come when you will be scattered, each to your own home. You will leave me all alone. Yet I am not alone, for my Father is with me. He was led like a lamb to the slaughter: And like a sheep that before its shearers is mute, so he opened not his mouth."

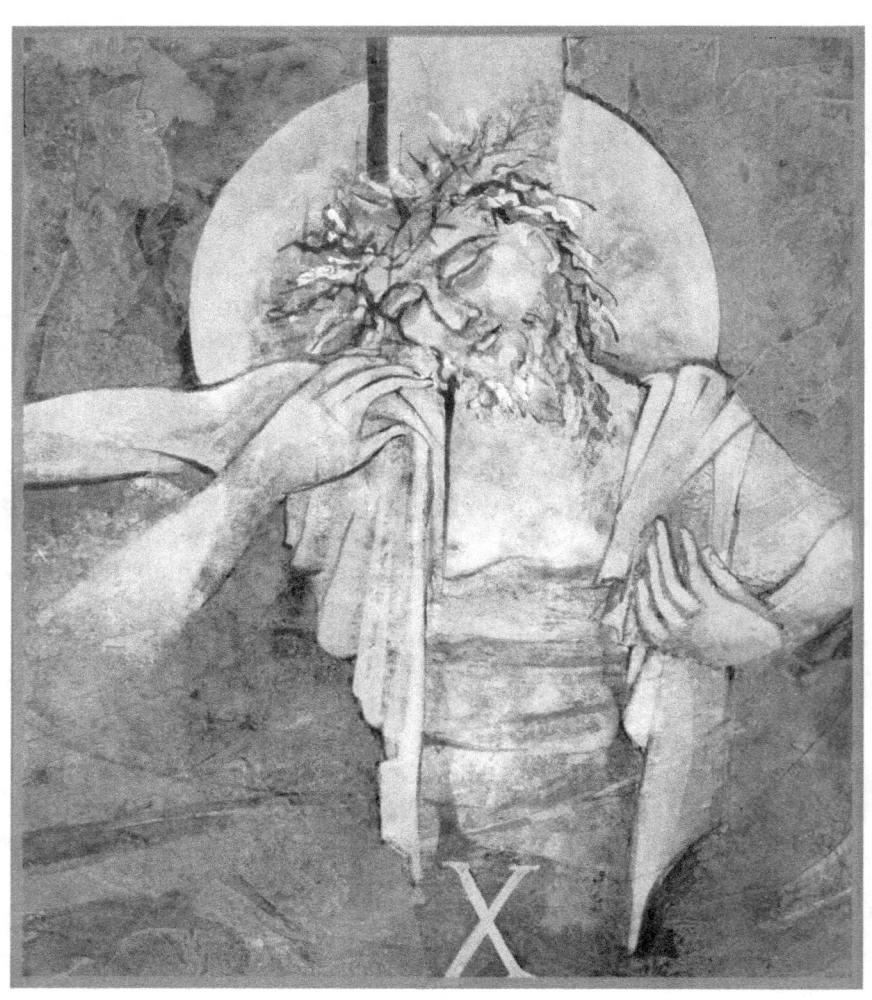

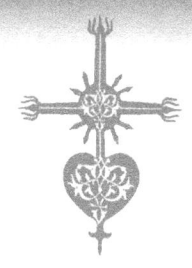

STATION 10

Jesus is Stripped of His Garments

WE ADORE YOU, O Christ, and we bless you.
BECAUSE BY YOUR HOLY cross you have redeemed the world.

His skin is raw and bruised like a used garment. Everything has been taken from him. He is stripped naked before everyone to see. Jesus has been condemned, beaten, made to drag his cross through the crowd of onlookers. He is going to be nailed to the cross. He has no physical or mental identity left with which to be bound to this earthly realm. No one seems to be willing or able to stop the progression of this unfolding horror.

By Station 10, the pain seems to pause and switch from the physical brutality to mental humiliation. Up until this point the robe protected his vulnerability from a crowd of onlookers. Being stripped naked publicly opens a floodgate of shame. There is nowhere to hide at this point. Jesus knows this is it. By exposing his skin and flesh to everyone, we see his humanness. We are the onlookers thrilled at seeing Jesus skin, the weak flesh full of sin like every other man. How can we believe this is the Son of God, the Savior, or King of Jews?

They gave me gall to eat. And when I was thirsty they gave me vinegar to drink.

> *Lord God, whose blessed Son our Savior gave his body to be whipped and his face to be spit upon, give us grace to accept joyfully the sufferings of the present time, confident your glory shall be revealed. Amen.*

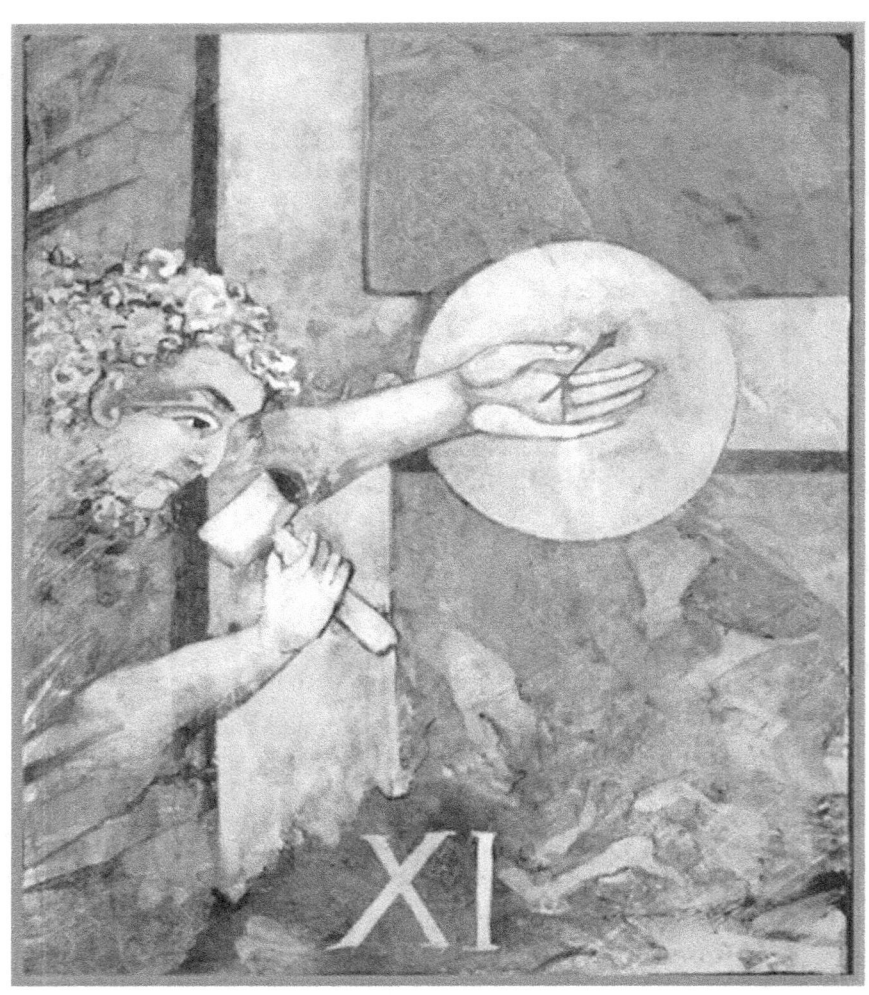

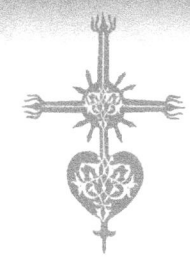

STATION 11

Jesus is Nailed to the Cross

WE ADORE YOU, O Christ, and we bless you.
BECAUSE BY YOUR HOLY cross you have redeemed the world.

Huge nails are hammered through his hands and feet to fix him on the cross. He is bleeding much more seriously now. As the cross is lifted up, the weight and power of life hangs on those nails. Every time he struggles to pull himself up to breathe, his ability to cling to life slips away a bit more.

After the horror of injustice, the physical suffering and naked humiliation, he is literally nailed to a common tree. He hangs on those nails as his life is poured out, shedding the last remaining drops of blood. Any snapshot image only captures a hint of the horror of a crucifixion. Can you bear to imagine even one small nail going through any part of you? Jesus can and does enter our life completely if we say, "Yes," to following his way. But this is beyond what most of us are willing to even consider. Has there ever been such surrender in anyone else that we might follow? Can there be any pain or agony of ours he would not understand?

Hebrews 13:5: "Keep your lives free from the love of money and be content with what you have, because God has said, 'Never will I leave you; never will I forsake you.' They pierce my hands and my feet: They stare and gloat over me."

> *Lord Jesus Christ, you stretched out your arms of love on the hard wood of the cross that everyone might come within the reach of you: so clothe us in your spirit that we, extending our arms in love, may come to know you to the knowledge and love of you. Amen.*

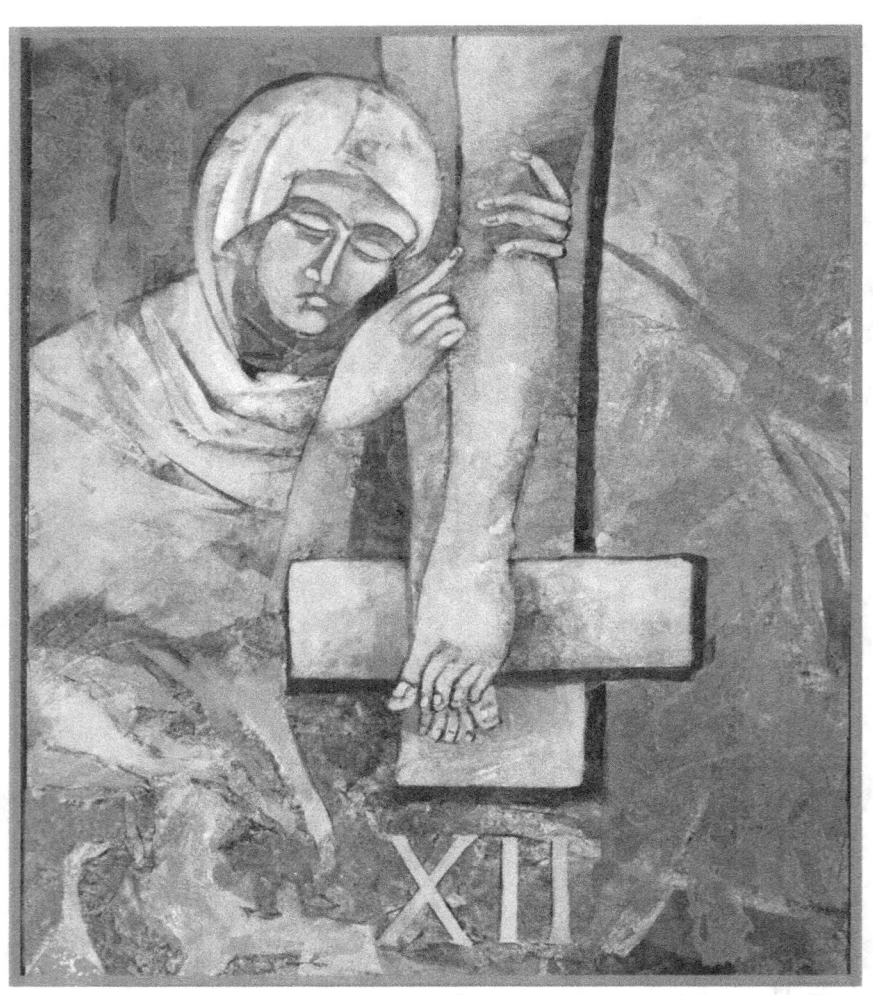

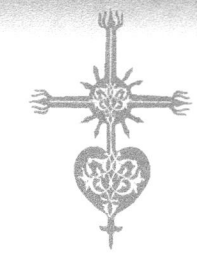

STATION 12

Jesus Dies on the Cross

WE ADORE YOU, O Christ, and we bless you.
BECAUSE BY YOUR HOLY cross you have redeemed the world.

Luke 23:34: "'Father, forgive them, for they do not know what they are doing.' And they divided up his clothes by casting lots. Imagine the love it takes to think of others after you have nothing left for yourself yet you still have the strength to forgive. Between two criminals, the two extremes mirrored in humanity, the one who is stubborn and self righteous, and the other who sees his faults clearly and humbly requests to be 'remembered in paradise' A mocking title above his head, INRI, might it better say 'Here hangs the King of Compassion and Mercy.' Jesus surrenders his last breath: 'Into your hands I commend my spirit.'"

Just moments before, Mary waited for the crowds to thin and for access to reach up to touch his nailed feet. Lightly holding the bottom of his foot, cheek against bruised and broken toes, she kisses his most vulnerable foot, thanks him and says goodbye. He is hanging still and lifeless, moments after his death. He has begun his transformation from physical form to merge with the universe. He still resembles the person he was just prior to death but all his flawlessness has changed into spirit, leaving behind what we might think of as only a shell or container.

Christ for us became obedient unto death, even death on a cross.

> O God, grant us the power to forgive, that we may ever more live with Christ in the joy of his resurrection. Amen.

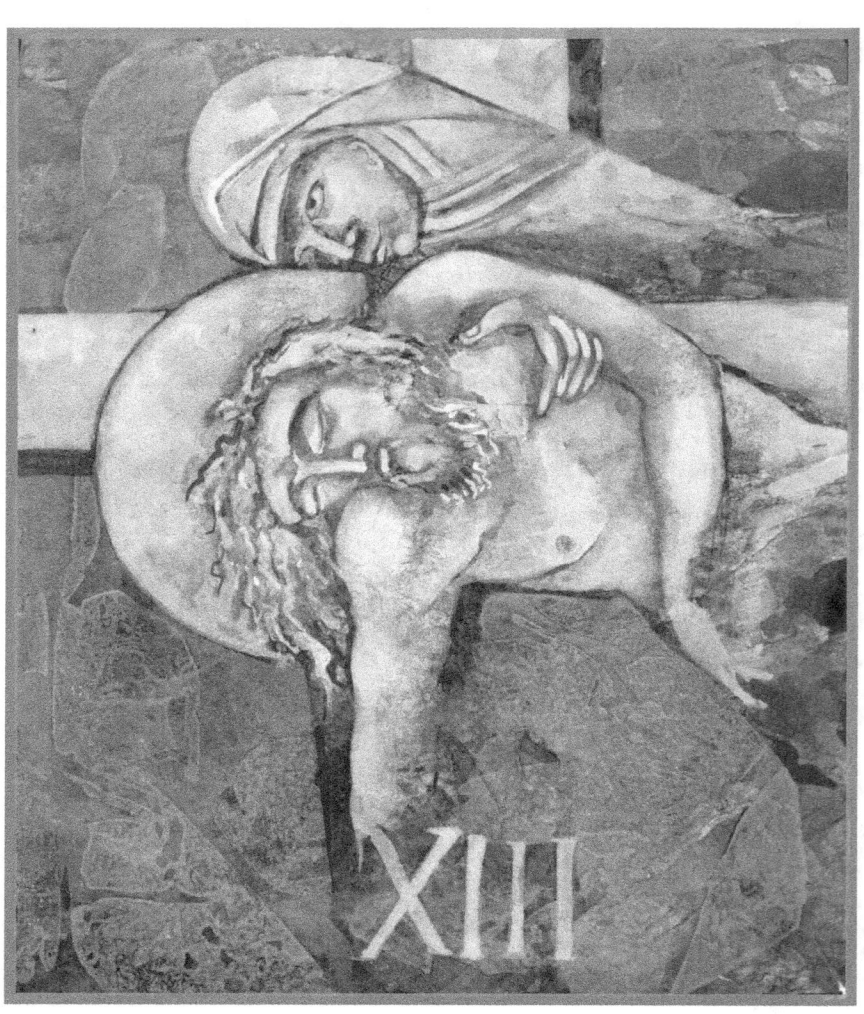

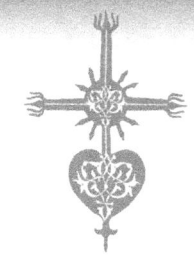

STATION 13

His Body is Laid on the Lap of His Mother

WE ADORE YOU, O Christ, and we bless you.
BECAUSE BY YOUR HOLY cross you have redeemed the world.

Here is tenderness and the absolute end. It is finished. The consequences of his journey have not been revealed. Yet there is no more to see, no more drama nor pain. It is over. The landscape is quiet. No action is called for. Joseph of Arimathea and Nicodemus went to Pilate to request Jesus' body. They wrapped the body in strips of linen and mixed in myrrh and aloe. Pilate requested that the tomb be sealed and a guard posted for three days in response to Jesus' assertion that he would rise after three days.

Seeing their immense grief stimulates us to reflect on the mystery of death. As he is taken down from the cross into the arms of Mary his Mother, Mary Magdalene and John, they are touching and caressing his body. During his short time of earth, his hands touched, blessed, healed and embraced the human condition in a wide variety of forms and circumstances. Now beneath their caresses, he has fallen entirely into God's hands.

Her tears run down her cheeks. And she has none to comfor her.

> *Lord Jesus Christ, by your death you took away the sting of death: grant to us your servants so to follow in faith where you have led the way, that we may be led into new life and wake up in your likeness; for your tender mercies's sake. Amen.*

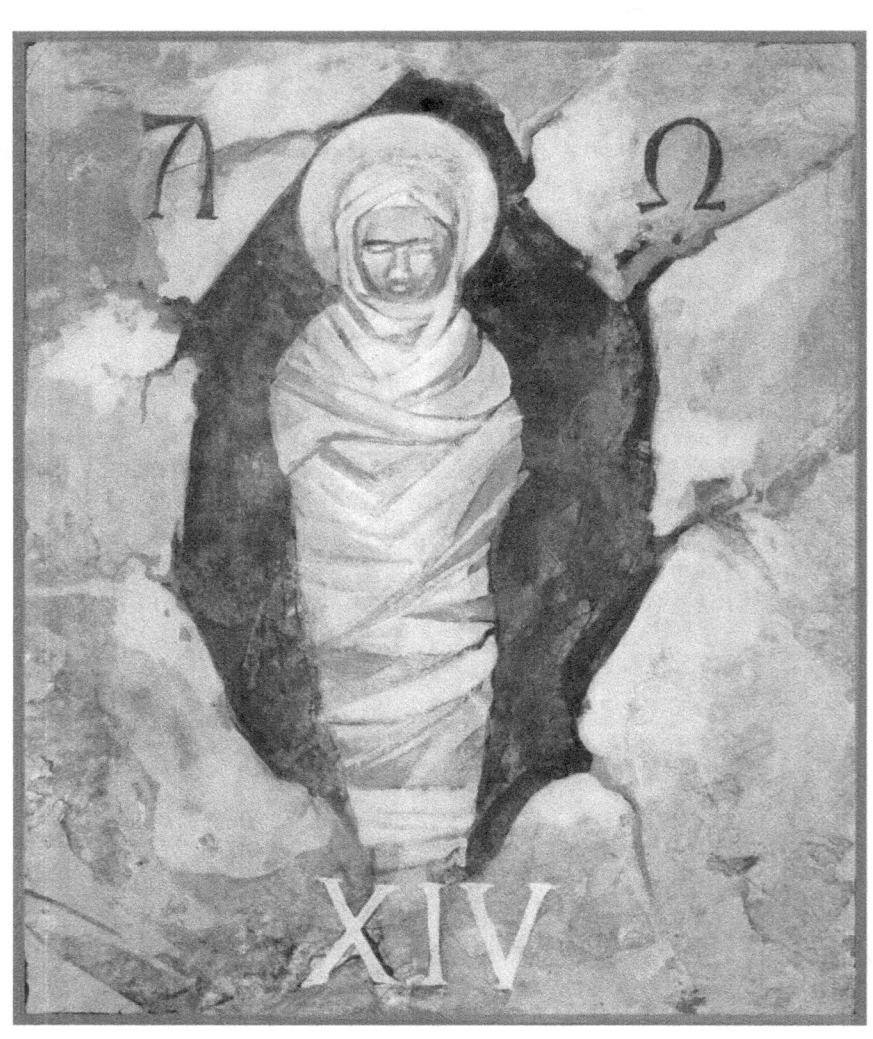

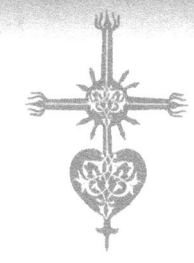

STATION 14

Jesus's Transfigured Body

WE ADORE YOU, O Christ, and we bless you.
BECAUSE BY YOUR HOLY cross you have redeemed the world.

They take the body of Jesus to its final resting place, or at least that is what they think. The huge stone over the tomb is the final sign of our human desire to make death permanent and complete. The soldiers think they can confine his being and body in a small tomb carved out of stone. In this final act, the soldiers try to ensure their dominance over him. They try to protect or defend that which is lifeless.

Who would have imagined the next day this tomb would be empty or that Jesus would show himself alive to his disciples, or that they would recognize him in the breaking of bread? The story cannot end in the tomb; it ends in each and every one of us sharing in his transfigured self.

Mark 9:2: "After six days Jesus took Peter, James and John with him and led them up a high mountain, where they were all alone. There he was transfigured before them. 'You will not abandon me to the grave: Nor let your holy one see corruption.'"

> *O God, your Son was laid in a tomb to rest, in quiet darkness: grant that we who have been buried with him through our baptism, may we find continual renewed and perfect peace in you. Amen.*

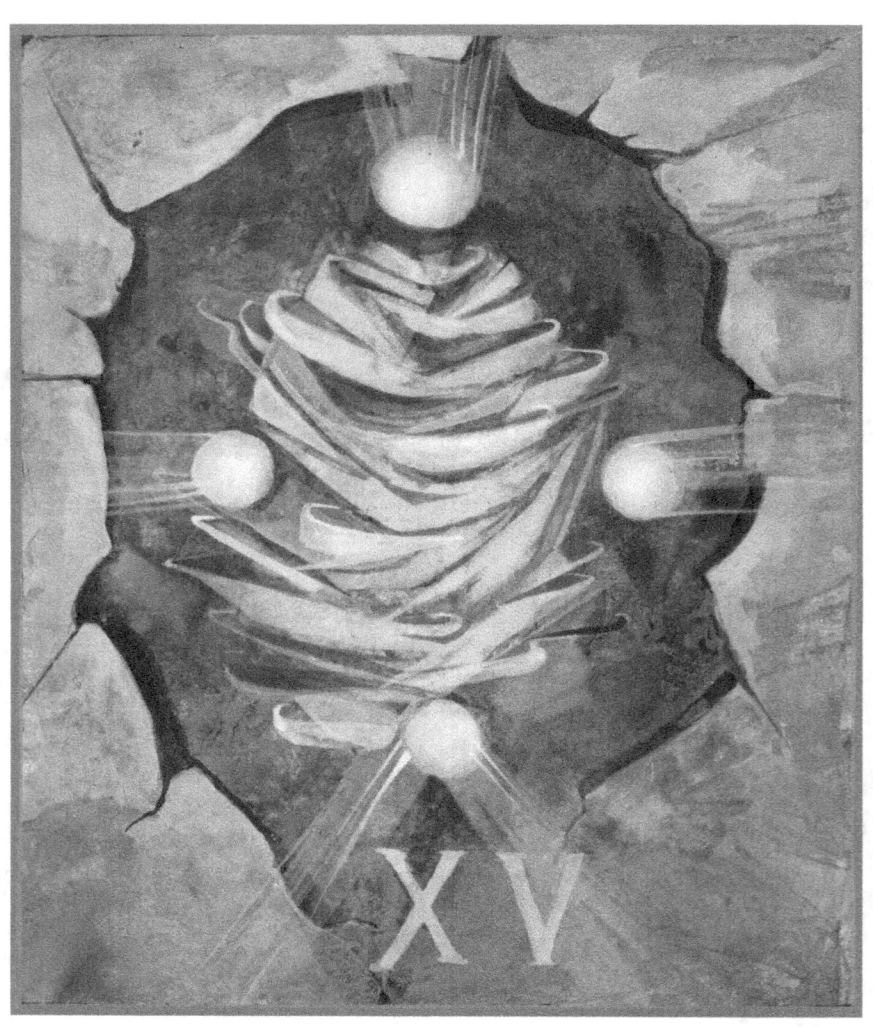

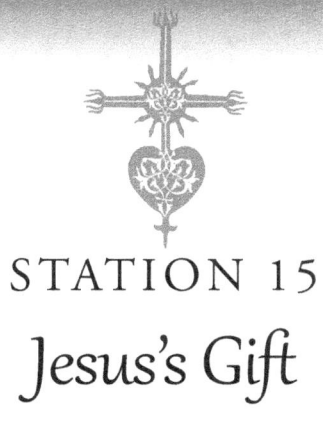

STATION 15

Jesus's Gift

We adore you, O Christ, and we bless you.Because by your holy cross you have redeemed the world.Oh, that our hearts might burn within as we realize how he had to suffer and die so as to enter into his glory for us. He is, and always has been, beyond us and everywhere. He is the light of the world.

He is the beginning and end of consciousness. He is no longer located in the tomb, the same way quantum physics is saying there is no time nor space.We are energy. We have always been energy. Yet we believe we are unique and special in this one life, imagining it is our own. Christ has changed all of that thinking. His gift from beginning to end is reminding us we own nothing. He showed us he owned nothing. Love is all there is. It is everywhere, to be seen first in Christ. All we have to do is look and not turn away from the suffering or horror happening around us.

His journey defies the idea of hatred and replaces it with eternal love. For love we have been created, and in Christ we see how to be that love without ownership of life or fear of death.

John 8:12: "When Jesus spoke again to the people, he said, 'I am the light of the world. Whoever follows me will never walk in darkness, but will have the light of life.' Savior of the world, by your cross and precious blood you have redeemed us: Strengthen us and help us to understand more deeply your ways, in Christ's name we pray."

> *We hank Christ our Lord who loves us and made us a kingdom of priests to serve his God and Father. To him be glory and dominion for ever and ever.Amen*

About the Author

Mary Jane Miller, born 1954 in New York has been a full time artist and thinker her entire life, and dedicated to iconography for the past 25 years. She resides in San Miguel de Allende, Mexico.

15 Stations of the Cross (Limited series) by Mary Jane Miller on Fine Art America

A poster of the complete collection of these 15 Stations is available on line. Useful for Individual devotions or make the collection of the individual egg tempera images a gift for your congregation. Mediate on the cross, and walk prayerfully.

fineartamerica.com/featured/15-stations-of-the-cross-mary-jane-miller.html

Other published works

In Light of Women her latest icon collection created as an exploration of women's image in iconography and their voices in the church. Vibrant text describing each images history, religious context and her own reflections about the world we live in today.

Icon Painting Technique, A Meditation and Guide to Egg Tempera explains the subtle relationship between the process of icon painting and how it reflects and enriches ones spiritual life.

The Mary Collection This collection of Mary icons captures the mysteries of the Madonna, drawing attention to the relationship between Mary and Christ, and the viewer. A wide range of imagination and potential is explored this tiny book.

Ancient Image, Sacred Lines are icon templates for painting and drawing. Each drawing is a meditation for healing or a template for iconographers.

One Mind, One World is a coloring book with line drawings from The Dialogue—an art installation with images of great religious leaders and philosophers, which promotes peace on earth and the idea we are all one.

Books can be purchased on Lulu.com and Amazon.com.

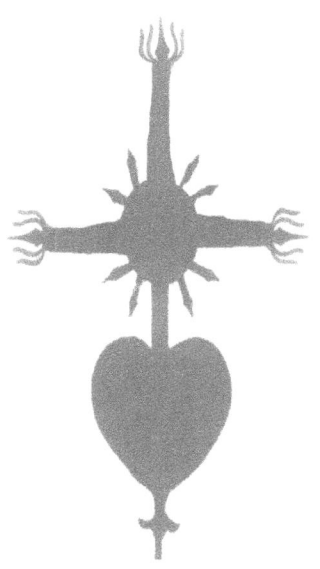

www.ingramcontent.com/pod-product-compliance
Lightning Source LLC
Chambersburg PA
CBHW030039230526
45472CB00002B/592